BEDTIME AT THE ZOO

BY EVIE BILLINGSLEY

Illustrated by Jason Velazquez

Bedtime at the Zoo
© 2025 by Evie Billingsley
Illustrated by Jason Velazquez

Printed in the United States of America.

ISBN Paperback: 979-8-9914263-3-6
ISBN Hardcover: 979-8-9914263-4-3

Billingsley Books
Fayetteville, Arkansas

Billingsley
BOOKS

Hi! My name is Ada, and I am the new zookeeper here at the zoo.

During the day, the zoo is a peaceful place where all kinds of animals live together in harmony.

But Oliver, the daytime zookeeper, warned me that sometimes the animals can become anxious at night.

Oliver gave me a list of the animals I need to tuck into bed.

First on my list are the gorillas. Wait. What is that noise? STOMP! STAMP!

Oh no! The gorillas are stomping and stamping on their brand new toys! What should I do?

I know! I'll check Oliver's list!

Breathing deep and slow should calm them down.

Breathe innn ... and ouuut... innn... and ouuut...

It worked! Now they are fast asleep.

Second on my list are the crocodiles. Wait. What is that noise?

"WAAAH! WAAAH!"
Oh no! The crocodiles are crying! What should I do?

I know! I'll check Oliver's list!

They must miss Oliver! Reassuring them that they are okay should calm them down.

Don't worry guys! You are okay, and Oliver will be back in the morning when you wake up!

It worked! Now they are fast asleep.

Third on my list are the hippos. Wait. What is that noise? SPLISH! SPLASH!

Oh no! The hippos are splashing muddy water everywhere! What should I do?

I know! I'll check Oliver's list!

Getting their energy out should calm them down.
Let's have a race!

On your mark...get set...GO!

It worked! Now they are fast asleep.

Last on my list are the zebras. Wait. What is that noise?

AHHHH! AHHHH!

Oh no! The zebras are scared after having bad dreams! What should I do?

I know! I'll check Oliver's list!

Giving them a warm, comforting hug should calm them down.

Don't worry! It was just a dream. I'm here for you. It worked! Now they are fast asleep.

I did it! All of the animals on Oliver's list are tucked into bed! I wonder why they were so restless.

Change is hard, and having a new zookeeper around must be uncomfortable. Luckily, I had Oliver's list to help me.

With some deep breaths, reassurance, exercise, and comfort, I was able to calm down the animals and tuck them into bed.

Hopefully, tomorrow night will go smoothly, but I know what to do if the animals need my help.

www.ingramcontent.com/pod-product-compliance
Ingram Content Group UK Ltd.
Pitfield, Milton Keynes, MK11 3LW, UK
UKHW050245150225

455113UK00014B/84

9 798991 426336